Propose, Prepare, Present

Alistair Croll

T0339225

O'REILLY®

Beijing · Cambridge · Farnham · Köln · Sebastopol · Tokyo

Propose, Prepare, Present

by Alistair Croll

Printed in the United States of America.

Published by O'Reilly Media, Inc., 1005 Gravenstein Highway North, Sebastopol, CA 95472.

O'Reilly books may be purchased for educational, business, or sales promotional use. Online editions are also available for most titles (*http://my.safaribooksonline.com*). For more information, contact our corporate/institutional sales department: (800) 998-9938 or *corporate@oreilly.com*.

February 2013:   First Edition

Revision History for the First Edition:

2013-05-28:   First release

See *http://oreilly.com/catalog/errata.csp?isbn=9781449366377* for release details.

ISBN: 978-1-449-36637-7

[LSI]

Table of Contents

Foreword

I did the math recently, and I've probably reviewed 10,000 conference submissions in my life. Each event I run gets 300 to 600 submissions a year, and I run at least four events each year. I've been at this for more than a decade.

On the one hand, that's a lot of terrible proposals to mine for just a few nuggets of content. On the other hand, many of those conferences have gone from nascent topics to prominent parts of the technology landscape, with a corresponding improvement in the quality of topics and calibre of speakers.

What's not obvious to outsiders is the amount of work that goes on behind the scenes: massaging content, shepherding speakers, wrangling slides, adjusting mics, tweaking websites, fixing registration SNAFUs, scouting venues, and marketing the events.

Running a conference is only slightly more complicated than planning a land invasion, and the people who make it run smoothly are the unsung heroes of the conference world. You'll make their jobs far easier if you suggest awesome content, follow through on your commitments, and invest time in surprising and delighting your audience. Hopefully this book will show you how to do that.

TL;DR: 22 Things to Remember

This book goes into a lot of detail. You may not have time to read it all, and you may not care how conferences are run or what their processes involve. You're more likely to be chosen if you read all of the material contained within this book, but if you're really in a rush, the part you must absolutely read is Chapter 3. It lists eleven things you should include, and eleven things you should avoid, to maximize your chances of acceptance.

Eleven Things to Include

- An inside recommendation from someone the organizers trust
- Sample videos and reviews showing how awesome you've been in the past
- A speaker who's a minority, all else being equal
- A clear explanation of who should attend and what they'll get out of it
- Alignment with the narrative the organizer is trying to create
- Indications that you'll be entertaining as well as informative
- An understanding of big trends without a platitude-laden presentation
- Personal stories from end users that humanize the content
- A willingness to adjust your format and topic to create something awesome
- Making it about something else tangentially related to the theme
- Opening the kimono and disclosing some secrets

Eleven Things to Avoid

- Vendor salesmanship and proposals that suggest you'll pitch
- Incomplete submissions or forms riddled with errors
- Not including a speaker's coordinates; using PR as an obstacle
- Jargon that won't be easy for readers to grasp
- Sounding like SkyMall, with outsized claims of uniqueness
- Trying to change content or speakers at the last minute
- Expecting to be paid or have travel paid for
- Proposing a subject too narrow to capture an audience's attention
- Bad spelling, formatting, and punctuation in your submission
- Submitting a book rather than a simple outline

- A bad past experience

Preface

Introduction

Every year, thousands of conferences happen around the world. Tens of thousands of companies—from industry giants to aspiring upstarts —jockey for their moment in the limelight, submitting presentation ideas and chasing organizers. They pump millions of dollars into these conferences, hoping to find new customers, strengthen their brand in the marketplace, and meet new partners.

Despite modern advances in technology, there's no substitute for the genuine contact of a face-to-face interaction or the serendipity of lobby networking. Conferences and events are big business, and done right, participation in an event can vault a company to the forefront of its market.

Yet for hundreds of companies, things don't go that way. Submitted topics aren't chosen, and when they are, they come across as tone-deaf sales pitches that alienate the audience and undermine all of the hard work done by organizers and presenters.

I'm hoping to change this. With the help of some of the smartest conference organizers from a dozen different events, I'm going to lay out what it takes to be chosen and how to make your presentation memorable and effective.

Apologies in Advance

This document may be a bitter pill to swallow, particularly for traditional marketers who expect their company to stay "on message" and who want to control a one-way monologue with their target market.

That world is over. In an era of social networks and immediate feedback, a one-way, controlled attitude is outdated and unsustainable. Conversations go where they will, and you need to throw out the monologue in a two-way world.

I'll also cite examples (with names changed to protect the innocent) in an attempt to better explain what works and what doesn't. Apologies in advance if you recognize yourself. I'm doing this to try and make things better for organizers, vendors, and presenters—and, above all, for audiences.

Ultimately, all of the suggestions and observations in this document come down to one thing: *figure out how to be interesting*. That's a difficult task to do well, but if you succeed, your efforts will be hugely rewarded.

Who This Is For

If you've got something to say, if you're a speaker, a PR/marketing person tasked with securing speaking slots, or if you're a speaking consultant specializing in executive speaker placement, then this book is for you. It'll show you why conferences are run the way they are, how to work with organizers, and what to do to make your participation successful.

CHAPTER 1

The Conference Industry

We can't talk about how to submit, create, and deliver great presentations without understanding how those presentations will be given. There are many different event formats out there, each with its own goals and business models.

Every conference is at a different place in the life cycle of its subject matter: some are exploring nascent subjects in the hopes of defining them, and others are reviewing well-worn material and focusing on practical applications of the topic.

Two Key Dimensions that Define a Conference

There are different kinds of events; it's important to distinguish them. Two important dimensions to consider are *where the content comes from* and *how the event is paid for*, as shown in Figure 1-1. These concepts drive how speakers are selected and what the topics will be.

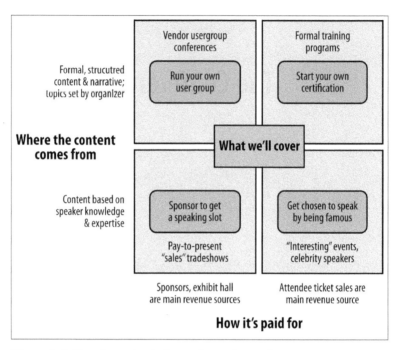

Figure 1-1. *Two important dimensions of a conference*

These two dimensions are useful because they explain the four basic conference types: vendor-run user groups, formal training programs, pay-to-present tradeshows, and pay-to-attend seminars. For each of these four types of event, organizers think about their content differently.

- A **vendor user group conference** generally involves end-user training and is run to maintain user loyalty, train users, and help ecosystem partners. Examples of this include Microsoft's MIX conference, Dreamforce, Android Open, VMworld, and Oracle World. The majority of the funding comes from sponsors (and the company itself), and the schedule is decided largely by the organizers and thus reflects their agenda.

- On the other hand, a **pay-to-present "sales" tradeshow** is paid for by sponsors, who get to speak about whatever they want. These events have little separation between content and money, so the stage is usually a series of presentations about each vendor's offerings. Attendance is cheap because attendee tickets are usually free or easily available. The content may be driven more by partisan agenda than speaker expertise; nevertheless, such events can be a useful way to spread knowledge and collect leads.

- A **formal training program** like the old Business Communications Review courses on WAN communications, or a CISSP security designation, or the Pragmatic Marketing training on product management, are often subsidized by an employer and can get the attendee a higher salary or better job prospects. Executive MBAs also fit into this category.

- Finally, the **"interesting" events with celebrity speakers** are attendee-paid, speaker-chosen conferences that lack formal structure. TED, The Lobby, Summitseries, and Web 2.0 Summit are good examples of this. Ticket prices are high, even to the point of creating prestige and exclusivity. The presenters are famous—or interesting—enough to speak on whatever they choose. Generally, there's no submission process: speakers are found based on the personal networks of the organizers and alumni and newsworthy events.

In reality, every event is a blend of these—some free events have a sponsor who says a few words; some vendor user groups have an exhibit hall; some formal programs include "unconference" tracks with less structure alongside their more rigid schedule; and invite-only "interesting" events are more like speed dating than education, using scarcity and celebrity to drive up ticket prices and focusing as much on surprising experiences, networking, and extra-curricular activities as they do on content.

It's also important to note that some conferences, particularly academic ones, don't fall neatly into this model. In those, presenters are chosen by peer review based on merit. But much of this book still applies to such events, because there's still a planning and judging process to understand.

The events that appeal most to for-profit companies are those with a reasonably structured format (so that the topics they care about are covered) and with content for which an audience pays (because when ticket prices are higher, attendees tend to be higher-level employees and executives with signing authority).

These events fall somewhere in the middle of Figure 1-1. For this kind of event, organizers often have a theme and narrative in mind. There's an advisory board, a formal call for papers, and a review process.

O'Reilly Web 2.0 Expo, Strata, and Velocity are examples of this format, as are conferences like Interop and industry association events such as CMG and eMetrics. It's this group of events I'll be talking about in the rest of the document, though the lessons covered here are useful for any kind of public appearance at which you want to engage the audience and be remembered.

 Festival-format events like Mutek, Decibel, South by Southwest (SXSW), or the Edinburgh Fringe Festival are hybrid events at which speakers are a blend of those who submitted and those whom companies pay to sponsor the programs or surrounding events. If you're submitting a proposal to them, then what you'll read here should help.

Because these events have both executive-level audiences (with the authority to make purchases) and a specific topic or segment of an industry, it costs a lot to buy a sponsored speaking slot. Being *chosen* to speak, on the other hand, costs nothing. An investment in the right submission and the right presentation pays handsome returns. Furthermore, if your company is exhibiting at the event, interesting presentations contribute to better booth traffic and more leads.

 Conference veteran Bob Goyetche points out, "As conference planning becomes easier, there's a whole movement of community-driven events (the *-camps, some *-fests, etc.) that feature very engaged participants not led by a vendor or platform. The possible returns of speaking at such events can be handsome as well." Grassroots events, even those with little or no admission cost, tend to fit in the bottom-right corner of Figure 1-1.

The Life Cycle of an Event

All topics have a natural ebb and flow. The best way to understand how an organizer is thinking about a conference is to look at the subjects that are discussed, the materials that are distributed, and the audiences that attend the event. Conferences and events happen because there's information to share, but the *kind* of information that's being shared depends on the life cycle of the event.

Figure 1-2 shows these stages, along with the subjects covered and materials you'll see.

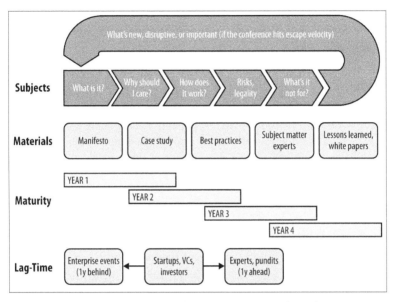

Figure 1-2. The evolution of conference content as the subject matures

A conference starts when an entirely new topic reaches critical mass. The pent-up interest in the subject grows until there's a group willing to come together, either organically (as an "unconference") or formally (within an industry or trade association such as the Web Analytics Association or the Computer Measurement Group). In technology, for example, this happened at the advent of mainframes (CMG), client-server computing (Interop), web protocols (Web 2.0 Expo), and cloud computing (Cloud Connect). But it's true of any new subject.

Stage One: What Is It?

In the early days, much of the event is devoted to defining what things are, agreeing on terminology, and providing metaphors and connections to well-known models so that people can understand the subject. Whether this is a Tea Party campaign comparing fiscal policy to a tax on tea or a cry for increased scientific funding that recalls the Dark Ages, appeals to history are often useful.

The best presentations tend to look like James Burke's *Connections*,[1] weaving history and speculation together into a whole and providing convenient metaphors with which to familiarize the subject. Nicholas Carr's *The Big Switch* framed the discussion of cloud computing; Clay Shirky's *Here Comes Everybody* and Don Tapscott's *Wikinomics* did the same for enterprise collaboration.

In the early stages of a topic, branding is done with cool names and memorable logos.

The Big Data industry, circa 2010, sounds like the cast of a comic book—Hadoop, Cassandra, Pig, Mongo, Basho. Proponents rally around technology stacks rather than applications or industries.

You'll also see more manifestos and fewer white papers at this stage. Provocation and controversy are the lifeblood of the industry, with Big, Hairy, Audacious Goals[2] around which to gather supporters.

At a 2007 hackathon, a friendly rivalry between Python and Rails developers devolved into a snowball fight that was a highlight of the event.

Stage Two: Why Should I Care?

Once there's a reasonable understanding of a topic and the ley lines of discussion are in place, audiences start to ask *why* instead of *what*. They're eager for practical applications and justifications because they need to decide whether to put the subject matter to work.

The discussion shifts from inflammatory manifestos and impassioned stump speeches, the discussion shifts to case studies and inside information on early adopters. It's all about justifying a move and over-

---

1. If you haven't watched *Connections* or *The Day The Universe Changed* yet, put this down and do so. It's an amazing example of how to tell stories in interesting and unexpected ways. See *http://www.youtube.com/user/JamesBurkeWeb*.

2. *http://en.wikipedia.org/wiki/Big_Hairy_Audacious_Goal*

coming the inertia inherent in any industry. This is what Geoffrey Moore referred to as *Crossing the Chasm*.

This is also the point at which enterprise customers start to pay attention because business cases for something start to materialize. Whether it's social media marketing, cloud computing, or how to flip real estate, once there's a *why*, there's a business discussion to be had.

Stage Three: How Does It Work?

Once the audience members know that the subject being covered is inevitable, they want to get their hands dirty. When social media was in its infancy, pundits opined on how it would transform our worlds. Later, marketers started to talk about the low barrier to entry, the return on investment (ROI) on social campaigns, and so on. But it took several years before they really wanted to understand how it functioned.

At this stage, workshops prevail. One thing organizers struggle with at this stage is the Paradox of Specifics[3]: audiences want concrete how-to information, but they don't want to be sold to. That leaves presenters with only a few options:

- **Speak at a generic level**. If you're at a hospitality conference, talk about how to deal with guests, but leave out the names of brands or tools you use.

- **Speak about the industry giants**. If there's a clear leader in the industry, then it's acceptable to discuss. Talking about search engine optimization? It's okay to mention Google.

- **Speak about free products**. If you're at a conference on blogging, then teaching WordPress is fine, because people can use it for free.

- **Do an "industry survey."** Compare how different vendors solve a particular problem, or what salaries are like within the attendees' professions.

This is a much bigger challenge to organizers than it might seem. Vendors want to showcase their product; audiences don't want to be sold to; and organizers want to move the discussion on to practical matters. Independent analysts can often get away with mentioning

---

3. Not a real paradox. But it sure makes it sound more important.

products and vendors, provided that they aren't seen as a shill for a particular offering.

Stage Four: Risks, Obstacles, and Legality

Now that the attendees know how something works, they want to know the challenges they'll face. Running a conference on buying and flipping houses? It's time to look at tax consequences, risks of mortgage defaults, and nightmare tenants. The audience is ready to start applying what they've learned in past years, but they want to mitigate as many of the common problems as possible by learning from others' mistakes.

Case studies work well here, and for vendors, a little humility and wound-licking is in order. Did it take you a while to figure out the right solution? Did a customer implementation go horribly wrong? Did you spend millions of dollars trying to sell something in the wrong way? Explain that. It's probably a better way to win hearts and minds than a product pitch.

Stage Five: What Can't I Use It For?

In the final stage of an event life cycle, there's a strange backlash. The pendulum of enthusiasm has swung too far in one direction, and now people want to find a healthy balance. Take cloud computing, for example: once audiences are convinced it's the right thing to do with all of your IT, they're fascinated by examples of what *doesn't* work in a cloud.

This is a transitional phase, at which the subject of the conference is now mainstream and the old ways are now the outliers.

Beyond: What's New?

For many conferences or events, this is the end. There's not enough "new" happening to create a critical mass around the subject matter. Everyone knows the subject, and they don't want to rehash the same old topics. The event turns into an annual reunion, and excitement drops.

Smart conference organizers anticipate this in stages three and four and try to extend the life cycle:

- They might branch out into new audiences, such as recent graduates, those hoping for a career change, or international versions of the event.
- They might divide the topic into more specialized segments (for example, a web analytics event could split into events focused on retailing, Software-as-a-Service, media, and mobility, allowing attendees to go deeper into each subject).
- They might create adjacent businesses—webinars, book imprints, or consulting offerings.
- They could organize regional events and membership groups, turning attendees into a community.
- They could create formal certification programs.
- They could align themselves with dominant vendors and become the user group event for a big firm with its own ecosystem.

Truly great conferences flourish because there's enough activity within their industry each year to generate new discussion. If the event has reached escape velocity, audiences will return each year to keep abreast of topics in their field. This kind of event may repeat popular content year after year and likely has tracks devoted to innovations within the field. Organizers worry less about finding new attendees and sponsors and more about encouraging alumni to return. They emphasize loyalty over acquisition. Feedback matters more and the attendees expect the organizers to chart their career path for them.

As we'll see, knowing where in this life cycle a particular conference is at lets you align a submission with the agenda that the organizers have for their event.

CHAPTER 2

From Idea to Stage: A Conference Timeline

All events go through the same basic stages of planning and execution. Understanding this cycle makes your submission more likely to get attention. Here's the life of a typical conference.

Topic Selection

Long before anyone hears about a conference, the planners are investigating the subject matter to see whether it's interesting and growing. They want to be sure there are enough people who will pay to attend and that the topics will continue to evolve so there will be new things to discuss in coming years.

If the conference has happened before, then the organizers will try to find a theme that focuses the subject matter somewhat, often around newsworthy events or major industry changes. For example, a real estate conference might choose the subprime mortgage crisis as a theme for that year's conference. Keynote speakers, artwork, and the kinds of presentations that will be chosen are all driven by this overarching narrative.

The event organizers are in business, too. They need to balance informative content that justifies the ticket price with provocation and entertainment that keeps people coming back. Achieving this kind of "edutainment" means choosing topics and speakers who are necessarily polarizing or controversial in order to provoke debate and discussion.

Organizers need to "skate to where the puck is going to be" by guessing what hot topics will be at the core of an industry well in advance of the mainstream. How far out this speculation goes depends on the attendees: academics and researchers can endure considerably more speculation than enterprise customers and risk-adverse executives.

 Edd Dumbill, chair of O'Reilly's Strata, points out that although organizers need to skate to where the puck is going to be, as those organizers become more established they can also have a hand in choosing where that puck is going to be. Bob Goyetche cites Oracle's OpenWorld, a vendor-driven event at which the company is specifically telling 45,000 attendees where they think the future lies.

Even if organizers don't formally declare a theme, they probably have one in mind. It's their job to anticipate where the industry is going and what audiences will be interested in—often a year in advance—so understanding how the organizers think is your first step in proposing a session that will be chosen.

Venue Selection

The size of the audience and the format of the event will dictate where it happens. Facilities impose many more constraints on a conference than attendees and presenters realize. The layout of a venue drives where exhibitors are, how many people can attend a keynote, how many concurrent sessions can run—even, in some states, how long unions say breaks between sessions must last.

Because venue contracts have to be signed well in advance, organizers often have to get creative with sponsorship models that depend on the facility itself. Proposing a nonstandard presentation could be a good thing: for example, if the elevators in the building have TV screens, maybe you could demonstrate interesting visualizations in the elevator cars. If you're at a conference on clean tech, perhaps you can supply water filtration, or carbon footprint calculation for the meals.

Getting creative with the venue and the organizers early on can introduce some variety into the conference.

Advisory Group

Many events have an advisory board of industry experts, analysts, prominent vendors, and end users. The role this board plays varies from conference to conference; sometimes it's purely ceremonial, but other times the board votes on submissions and helps to decide what topics should be covered.

Done right, an advisory group not only helps to keep the organizers honest but also serves as "forward-looking radar" for what's in store within a particular industry. Some conference organizers use tools to collect advisors' ratings of submitted talks and decide what sessions will be presented.

The advisory board may be publicly announced (in which case it's often a matter of prestige) or it may be a closely guarded secret (often to avoid harassment of the advisors by zealous marketers and PR agencies hoping to lobby for their clients). If it's a relatively new event, then the advisors can lend it credibility and provide structure and contacts. One of their first jobs will be to get the word out about the conference so that speakers submit topic suggestions.

Call for Presentations/Papers/Proposals (CFP)

At this point, the organizers have to come up with content. The degree of outside participation varies from event to event.

- For a formal, vendor-run event, it will likely be driven by the content that needs to be covered to obtain some kind of accreditation or training qualification.
- For a "celebrity" event like TED or Web 2.0 Summit, it will happen through personal networks (though TED does rely on regional TEDx events as a "farm team" and lets people suggest speakers).
- The organizers may supply an overarching theme and ask for submissions on this topic.
- If the event is organized into "themes" or "tracks," then submissions will be grouped into those categories. For example, a cloud computing conference might include tracks on security, public clouds, and building a business case.

The theme may be implied by the conference: an electronic music festival is going to solicit musicians, producers, and industry insiders, for example.

 In a CFP, I like to collect additional information about speakers, topics, and formats that will be used to judge submissions. This information may include videos of past presentations, biographies, LinkedIn profiles, Twitter accounts, and so on. The more complete and professional these things are, the greater your chances of making it through the selection process.

CFP Review

Once the CFP is ended, reviewers rate the submissions. This process varies from event to event, but it usually includes:

- A first pass at filtering sessions, based either on a group of reviewers' votes or an organizer's judgment. This process is when truly awful presentations—those that don't fit the theme or that are inappropriate or terribly written—get cut. Sometimes this process can be a public voting system open to the whole world or to registered attendees.
- A second review in which the person responsible for each track or theme looks at a shorter list of submissions that survived the initial gauntlet.
- Mailing some of the submitters for clarification or to offer them a chance to adjust their session title or content.
- Confirmation that the submitter can attend the event, possibly dealing with travel expenses or honoraria (though this is very unusual in events for which a speaker submits a topic).

Some organizations have sophisticated voting tools for this process; others use a simple shared spreadsheet or "top ten" lists.

What Are the Odds of Acceptance?

Conference organizers receive hundreds or even thousands of proposals. Those are competing for only a few speaking slots, and many slots will be filled by experts, pundits, or invited guests who were sought out by the organizers—or by sponsors who've paid to present.

Acceptance rates vary widely across events. We analyzed the number of submissions across all O'Reilly conferences in recent years and the total number of speaking slots available at those events, as shown in Figure 2-1.

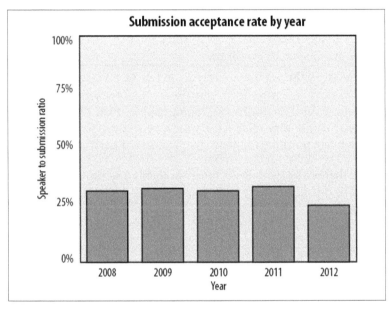

Figure 2-1. Submission acceptance rate by year

In other words, depending on the number of sponsors and invited speakers, you have a 15 to 30 percent chance of being accepted to speak at one of these events.

Narratives and Tracks

The organizers now pick a "grid" of tracks and topics. This step is more art than science; it's a combination of:

- **Physical constraints** such as the amount of time the venue is available or the number of rooms that can be used concurrently.
- **Winning submissions** from the CFP voting process that should be included.

- **Quotas and goals** such as including underrepresented groups; ensuring representation from different countries; making sure that at least half of the speakers work for startups; making sure each track has a debate and a panel; and so on.
- The **"hot topics"** that the organizers and advisors think will be important in the coming year.
- **Known good speakers or subject matter experts** contacted through personal networks or from past years.
- **Sales constraints** such as a sponsored track or intermittent "word from our sponsor" sessions.
- **The story the organizer is trying to tell**. Good events tell a story that takes attendees from one place to another, and occur in a natural "arc." Foundational topics happen first; talks about tomorrow are scheduled later. Controversies are surfaced on the first day; possible solutions are offered on the last one.

Before there's a final schedule, there's probably a working spreadsheet shared by organizers that outlines possible sessions and themes, which changes daily.

 One PR organization emailed me four times after the closing of the CFP to inquire about the status of the submission. Because the conference had clearly stated the date by which the schedule would be announced, their emails didn't add anything to the decision process.

I hadn't yet reviewed their proposal. But after reading their fourth email, I reviewed the submissions in question, admittedly with a more critical eye. I quickly realized that it was far more sales-oriented than I wanted. As a result, the speaker wasn't chosen. The lesson is that sometimes, pestering organizers exposes sessions to unwelcome scrutiny and can backfire.

Building a conference grid is a continuous process of balancing changing topics, last-minute cancellations, eager salespeople, and more egos than there are available slots. It's like planning wedding seating on an epic scale. If you want to know why conference organizers are perpetually grumpy or distracted, look no further than this.

Fitting Sessions to Tracks

Once the tracks are defined, it's a matter of picking the right ones to fit the narrative within each track. If there's a track chair, he or she will figure out the order and may adjust the session titles and descriptions to make it flow well. Great conferences worry a lot about copyediting.

The event organizers also work with the track chairs to prevent a lot of overlap between sessions happening at the same time (for example, two sessions on making fish lures or the music of Vivaldi probably shouldn't happen concurrently, because attendees won't know where to go).

The track chair may also change the format of the sessions—a simple presentation might become a one-on-one "fireside chat"; a panel discussion might turn into a formal debate. These are good ways to introduce variety into the event and keep audiences on their toes, and they can also help reduce the "salesmanship" that inevitably happens when vendors present.

Inviting Presenters

Armed with the list of presenters and formats, the organizers—or sometimes the track chairs themselves—invite speakers. At this point, organizers are assuming that all the people who've proposed sessions will be able to make it if they're confirmed.

One of the biggest irritants for event organizers is people who submit a session, then say they can't attend. This is a sure way to get blacklisted for future events, and organizers have a very long memory. I have a dozen past applicants I simply will never choose again because of this behavior.[1]

If a presenter can't make it, or isn't willing to adjust their topic or content, then the track chair goes to backup submissions. This is one of the reasons it takes so long to find out whether a session you've submitted has been chosen: you may be a backup, and the organizers may be waiting to hear back from a higher-rated submitter first.

---

1. Other people may be more forgiving.

Finalizing Titles and Descriptions

With all of the speakers confirmed, the event publishes its lineup on the conference site. This publication may happen gradually, as confirmations come in, or in order to build excitement, but the lineup is generally available months in advance so that the event can sell tickets.

During this time, the presenters work on their content. For some events, the presenters may also be asked to write guests blog posts, join Twitter lists, participate in online "preview" events, or otherwise engage with the burgeoning audience prior to the event itself.

Reviewing Presentations

Presenters have a deadline by which to get presentations in. If the subject matter of the event doesn't change much, this date may be weeks, or even months, in advance of the conference—particularly if the event organizers are publishing the presentations. In other cases, presentations may be delivered at the last minute.

Regardless of last-minute changes that are needed, event organizers want to see presentations beforehand:

- Not getting a presentation in on time is, in my experience, the single best early indicator of a problem speaker—someone who will cancel, try to switch slides at the last minute, sell from the stage, or try to substitute someone else.

- The slide deck itself shows whether the presenter will adhere to the content of their session.

- Slide compatibility issues are common. Presentations can be in PowerPoint, Keynote, Prezi, or PDF; they can be created on various operating systems, with various fonts, in various aspect ratios, and they may have embedded content that's hard to play. Resolving these issues early is essential.

- Organizers may be making slides available online, either as a password-protected download or on a public site such as Slide-Share. This takes time, and attendees expect content as soon as they leave the session.

Every year, at one of the events I run, the most common complaints organizers get from attendees is that content isn't available online as a download, despite the fact that the URL for content is in rotation on every screen in between sessions and attendees are mailed the link.

This is also a good time to let the organizers know about any special technical requirements. Will you want to present from your own computer so that you can review notes and see the upcoming slide in your deck? Unless you ask well in advance, the organizers probably won't be able to accommodate your requests.

The Event Itself

A few weeks beforehand, the event signage is printed. A couple of days before the event, organizers may print handouts or schedules. At this point, changes to speakers, bios, or session outlines *really* annoy organizers and may result in your session being cancelled.

Once onsite, speakers must check in with a ready-room or speaker services area. If you don't do this checkin, the organizers may not know you're on site.

At one prominent conference, a well-known analyst, superb speaker, and veteran presenter didn't check in with Speaker Services, choosing instead to register at general registration. He then went and sat in the audience to watch the proceedings.

Unfortunately, because none of the organizers knew he was around, we found a replacement for him at the last minute. He was surprised to hear us mention from the stage right in front of him that he wasn't able to make it—after all, he was only a few feet away —and didn't get to participate in the session for which he'd traveled so far.

When it's time for your session, you should probably go and be nice to the audiovisual (A/V) team. More than anyone else, these folks can make or break your presentation. They'll need to get you mic'd up and ensure that your slides are displaying properly. If you have any special requirements such as video, audio, or using your own computer—assuming these were approved earlier in the process—they're the ones who have to deal with it.

Follow-Up, Sharing, and Feedback

If you've given the audience ways to reach you—Twitter and email work fine—then follow up with them. Although it's not cool to sell from the stage, it's perfectly acceptable to give the audience a suggested way of following up, such as going to your website or visiting your booth.

Many events will share content online. Unless you have reasons not to do so, consider SlideShare, Paper.li, Scribd, or some other document-sharing platform that you can use to get your content into the hands of the audience.

You'll likely want to look at social networks for feedback, too. Checking the event hash tag and mentions of your name in all its formats will give you a sense of how things went. It's also an opportunity to answer detractors and befriend critics if you do it right: social media users love genuine, transparent responses.

A keynote presenter on the first day of a conference gave a tone-deaf 15-minute sales pitch. Before he was finished, Twitter lit up in protest with calls for him to get off the stage and complaints that attendees had spent money on the event and expected more from it.

The following morning, a second presenter—from a large, well-known, and notoriously risk-averse company—took the stage. Instead of starting with his slide deck, he paused, looked at the audience, and said, "I read Twitter, too. I was reading it yesterday. And as a result, I've thrown out most of my slides and I'm just going to talk."

It was a resounding success. He made his points anyway, the audience listened, and the Twitter peanut gallery praised him for his candor and directness.

CHAPTER 3

What Organizers Are Looking For

Now that you understand the hurdles a submission has to go through before it becomes a speaking gig, here's how to give yourself the greatest chance of success. Above all else, *be interesting and relevant to the organizers' narrative.*

It isn't easy to get inside the mind of an event organizer. Many of them don't know how they do what they do, as they're tapping into the zeitgeist of an industry or a subject. They may not like to show their cards —after all, conferences are a competitive business. At the very least, look at past events and which sessions were rated highly. Using your knowledge of the life cycle of a conference and the kinds of events in the industry, you're already ahead of the pack.

Eleven Things that Will Get You Chosen

The number-one rule for submitting content is to *respect the process* —the CFP, selection, and deadlines are there for very good reasons of which you may not be entirely aware. Here are some additional surefire ways to give your submission the best chance of being chosen.

Inside Recommendation

Above all, a recommendation from someone whom the organizers trust will ensure that you get looked at. Getting into a conference schedule is like applying for a job: without an introduction, you're just a résumé in a stack of papers.

There's a good reason that recommendations matter. It's hard to tell from a submission whether the presenter will be any good. Having someone else stick their neck out means at least one person vouches for the presenter's ability to engage and entertain a room.

Just because you're getting a recommendation doesn't mean you can skip the normal process. There must still be a submission in the system to attach the recommendation to. Within the proposal itself, it's absolutely appropriate to mention the recommendation or to let reviewers know that one of the organizers asked you to submit a session proposal.

There's no way to fake a recommendation. If the organizers don't trust the person who's recommending you—or if one of their past recommendations hasn't been good—that person's suggestion may actually hurt your chances. The selection of excellent speakers runs on a currency of trust. One DJ and promoter we know nurtures his army of smart contacts who suggest new music and new artists for him. He calls them his "truffle pigs." So the best thing you can do is find the organizers' truffle pigs, and convince them that your session is awesome.

Sample Videos and Reviews

The best indicator of someone's presenting ability is a video of them presenting. Organizers understand that videos are shaky, have poor audio, and don't show the slides alongside the speaker. We get that. But there's no substitute for seeing someone work the room. Do they read their notes, or walk with wild abandon? Do they extemporize, or stick to the script? Are they interacting with the audience, or delivering a monologue?

If the videos are posted publicly, then there will probably be audience feedback, which is even better. Ratings and information from others can help decide. For that matter, if a presentation goes really well, grab the Twitter feed containing the accolades—they're the next best things to testimonials.

A Speaker Who's a Minority

Many conferences have policies that favor women, minorities, or groups that aren't well represented within their industry. If your speaker conforms to such a policy, say so. For that matter, try and find a speaker who does.

 In one technology conference I run, roughly 1 percent of submitted speakers are women. Yet more than 10 percent of the people who take the stage are women. This doesn't happen by accident: we're actively trying to get women onstage in an industry in which they're seldom a part of the conversation.

After reviewing more than 300 submissions for another event—none of which featured female speakers—I appealed to Twitter. I got several great recommendations, all of whom are now part of the lineup.

There are few other things you can do that will give you a tenfold increase in your chance of being chosen. I'm not going to get into the politics of affirmative action here. Suffice it to say that speaker lineups should be representative of the population, and in many industries that isn't the case. Conference organizers want to fix this situation without compromising the quality of their content.

A Clear Explanation of Who Should Attend and What They'll Get Out of It

Often, it's unclear from a session description just who is supposed to be the audience. You can help by providing a list of who should attend and what they can expect to leave with.

List the types of job titles (product manager, software architect) or formal training (familiarity with current international tax law, ability to program in Java) of intended attendees. Also list things the attendees should bring (a working computer, a pen and paper).

Similarly, list *as quantitatively and factually as possible* what attendees will accomplish. Avoid superlatives and sales here: the more concrete, the better. Don't say "Attendees will understand the importance of social media"; say "Attendees will leave knowing how to set up profiles on four major social networks."

Remember, too, that your description has to sell. You're trying to convince attendees who are choosing which session to attend that your session is better than all the others. If they don't show up, you won't be invited back; if you fill the room, you're the first person the organizers will call next year.

Alignment with the Narrative the Organizer Is Trying to Create

If you're able to figure out what kind of story the event will tell, align your submission with it. Remember, much of the tone of content is driven by the life cycle of the event. Are we in the early stages of an industry? Then a bombastic, polarizing presentation may be in order. Later in the life cycle? Case studies and cautionary tales may work better.

If there are hot topics, mention them. Be careful to pick those that are novel enough to inspire curiosity, but still established enough that they'll fill a room. This is a tricky balance to strike because it means novelty alongside broad appeal.

Indications that You'll Be Entertaining as Well as Informative

Conferences are edutainment. It's impossible to make a point if nobody's listening; on the other hand, if you have the room's attention, they'll remember your message. So don't be boring.

One way to achieve this goal is to take a new angle on an old idea. Don't talk about computer security; talk about the impact of baby boomers' ailing eyesight on security. Don't talk about food safety; talk about the rise of "authentic" cooking. You need to be memorable before you can be informative.

Sometimes this approach backfires. Trying to use "hip" language can come across as forced, and this is where companies need to find people who are naturally engaging, regardless of their place in the organization, and put them forward.

Attendees often compare notes when deciding what to attend; they skip out of keynotes to make phone calls when they think the content won't be fun. So polarize, provoke, surprise, and inspire. If you can convey this attitude in your presentation, the organizers will be far more likely to choose you.

An Understanding of Macroscopic Trends without a Macroscopic Presentation

There's another paradox that presenters face: staying high-level while providing depth. Most companies either aim too high or too low. They offer boring platitudes ("now, more than ever, people are connected") or they get down in the weeds ("the XYZ 74 is 76 percent more juicy because of its flange-baffle").

Reporters have a way of dealing with this. Rather than reporting the news, the really good ones report on *why the news matters* and *what will happen as a result*. The rise of Twitter might be newsworthy, but it's the demise of cable news that's fascinating. The collapse of the Greek economy is the news, but it's how life changes for Athenians or what other countries collapse that's the story.

 I was once presenting a session on cloud computing. In his book *The Big Switch*,[1] author Nicholas Carr had drawn parallels between cloud computing and other utilities, such as the electrical grid.

Rather than talk more about the analogy, I decided to look at what happened once the grid was commonplace. What changed in the face of cheap, ubiquitous electricity? As it turns out, a few short years after the deployment of the electrical grid, the hot business was electrical appliances—which proponents claimed would revolutionize housework, a benefit that failed to materialize for a variety of fascinating reasons.

The presentation got great reviews, largely because it wasn't yet another cloud deck, but instead speculated on current trends in a new light.

The mark of great books is that they make the reader feel smarter for reading them. The same is true of great presentations: tying big-picture trends to current topics like technology, economics, philosophy, productivity, and humanity makes the audience feel smarter without getting caught in the weeds.

1. www.nicholasgcarr.com/bigswitch/ (*http://www.nicholasgcarr.com/bigswitch/*)

Contrast is also good. Organizers want balance: if the discussion at the conference focuses on big-picture issues (such as healthcare), you could present a session on how this will affect an individual (a grand-mother in Florida). On the other hand, if it's focusing on specifics (changes to the tax code for real estate), you could look at societal impacts (how tax changes have affected standards of living over the ages).

End Users

Good conferences have a healthy tension between the audience and the speakers. There has to be an imbalance of knowledge between the two for attendees to find it valuable. This is one of the reasons that professional groups' events are often dull: a realtor talking to other realtors about things everyone already knows is fun for no-one. Unless there's something to share, the content won't be well received.

In the early stages of a conference's life span, pioneers have a lot to share. They've taken risks, and as early adopters, their knowledge is valuable to those considering following in their footsteps. War stories from actual end users, customers, and mere mortals are always well received because the audience can relate to them and they're less likely to be sales pitches.

If you're submitting a topic, consider offering an end user instead. The more hard data the end user can share, the better. Perhaps he or she has a spreadsheet that was used to justify the business case, or some data on how well it worked. Anything the attendees can take away and apply to themselves is good.

Willingness to Adjust the Format and Topic

If your proposal is close to the mark, organizers may want to use it in another format. A three-hour workshop you propose might be better as a 45-minute session; the speaker you suggested might be a welcome addition to a panel. Or maybe the keynote topic you submitted won't fit, but there's something in your speaker's background that caught the eye of those planning the content.

In one case, I reached out to a speaker with an adjustment to her session outline because it didn't fit the intended audience and contained vendor-specific brands. Although she was eager to participate, subsequent rewrites and tweaks kept returning to the original topic and reintroducing the brands.

After three iterations, I gave up and found another speaker. Although the first choice was talented and had received accolades from other event organizers, we weren't able to align her topics to the audience or remove the salesmanship from the discussion.

Organizers have a show to put on, and the role you're cast in may not be the one you'd hoped for. But you're much more likely to play a part if you work with them to create a session that fits your expertise *and* their narrative.

Making It About Something Else

What's the most interesting thing in the world right now? Maybe it's a celebrity, or an election, or a humanitarian crisis, or the death of a public figure. Try submitting a proposal about that. In the context of that topic, how does your expertise affect it? How will your product change elections? What are the legal implications of the news? How does the crisis change real estate or the economic outlook?

Speaker consulting firm S3 tells its clients to frame the purpose of their talk in an interesting way, such as a story, questions, or statistics. Focus on educating the audience or helping them to solve a problem.

If your submission is about something else, people will remember it. And it will stand out when organizers select the topic.

Opening the Kimono

When all else fails, share a secret.

Most organizations eat their own dog food. A software company might use its own tools; a realtor might have sold their house recently; a lawyer might have an approach to preparing closing arguments; a service provider might have custom power management.

Everyone loves to see inside the kimono. If you can reveal secrets (within reason and corporate governance, of course), then do so. Specific numbers are even better, because the audience will be going through the same things themselves and you'll give them something to compare to.

Eleven Things that Will Get You Rejected

There are, of course, plenty of ways in which your submission will be rejected. Usually, this is simply a numbers game.

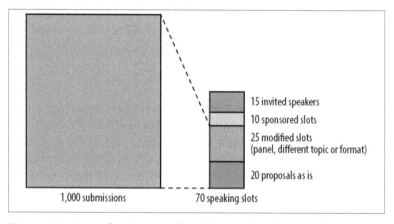

Figure 3-1. A rough estimate of a submission's chances of being chosen

Out of the hundreds of submissions, only a few will be used, as Figure 3-1 illustrates, and only a few more will be turned into different topics or invitations to participate. Although Figure 3-1 is a best guess across dozens of events, it's indicative of the triage organizers have to perform.

Conference veteran Jesse Robbins, a sought-after speaker who founded the Velocity conference before building OpsCode, suggests adding another turn-off: sessions proposed by a PR firm or marketing person. "If you want to speak at a quality event managed by organizers who care, submit the proposal yourself and manage the relationship yourself."

Doing some of the following things makes it easy to cross your submission off the list.

Vendor Salesmanship

Nothing will get you refused as fast as a sales pitch. This is the single biggest reason for rejection in every conference I've ever run, across dozens of topics and hundreds of reviewers.

 As one track chair remarked while digging through dozens of proposals, "If you mention your company's product name in your proposal, I'm pretty much going to ignore you."

We looked at the best-reviewed and worst-reviewed submissions from thousands of submissions submitted to O'Reilly's CFPs across five years and more than twenty events. We defined "good" as having the highest score from the most reviewers and "bad" as the lowest score from the most reviewers.

Then we built a tag cloud visualization of the words that appeared in reviewer comments—the more often the word appears, the bigger it is in the visualization.

Figure 3-2 shows what people said about the best-reviewed proposals.

Figure 3-2. Text from comments in the 500 best-reviewed submissions across several years of conferences

Figure 3-3 shows what they said about the worst-reviewed ones.

Figure 3-3. Text from comments in the 500 worst-reviewed submissions across several years of conferences

The results are pretty clear: good proposals are interesting, inspire emotions, and have both a great topic and a great speaker. On the other hand, bad proposals sound like product sales pitches.

Bob Goyetche reminded me that conference organizers often speak to one another.

"We once had one author blatantly disregard the 'don't sell' rule at one of our events. He even mentioned in his talk the fact that he was ignoring our request. We managed to usher him offstage rather quickly by completely dropping a planned Q&A with him and running an impromptu prize giveaway to bring the room back to life. Attendees weren't thrilled with him, but they appreciated how we handled it.

I've since had other conference organizers look at our past programs and ask how this individual's session went over. You can guess that my response included his disrespect for us and our audience. I hope that was worth it for him."

Copy and Paste with Bad Characters

Many CFP submissions are done through a web form. Those forms have constraints:

- The form may limit the number of characters to 400 letters, for example.
- For security reasons, the form may not accept certain letters and symbols.
- Certain fields may force the submitter to choose from a list.

If you're careless about submissions, it shows. Many PR agencies and marketing departments use the same boilerplate text and topics across dozens of events, essentially spamming all of the conferences on the circuit. Some even use tools to automate the process completely. The content therefore isn't tailored to a particular event or the narrative that organizers have in mind. Organizers hate this.

One way they can tell is that submissions run afoul of the constraints imposed by the form. Text is cut off mid-sentence; drop-down fields haven't changed from their defaults; strange characters show up in the text. With hundreds of submissions to read through, an unreadable or incomplete submission will be rejected—particularly if it makes the reader think it's simply part of a bulk submission across many events.

Not Including the Speaker's Coordinates

Another habit of PR agencies and speaker bureaus is to omit the speaker's contact information. To understand why this happens, you need to know how agencies get paid.

Agencies and speaker bureaus are constantly under pressure to demonstrate their value to clients. They want credit for every article, reference, retweet, and speaking engagement so their clients will renew their service contract; in some cases, they may even get paid per event in which they place a speaker. By forcing organizers to contact them, they can stay in the loop and take credit for their work.

This drives us insane. As organizers, we care only about the speaker and his or her ability to connect with a crowd. If we can't connect with the speaker, we're likely to pass. We'll happily copy an agency and work with them on logistics—but if you submit someone for a session, you'd better include their contact information.

 A global telecommunications company had been complaining repeatedly that its speakers weren't selected for a conference, despite flooding the CFP with dozens of ideas.

In the third year of the event, the company offered a great speaker and a compelling topic, and I chose it. But the contact information wasn't in the submission, and the PR person didn't respond to repeated requests for an introduction.

The result? We chose a competitor of theirs who was more than happy to fill the spot and to teach a similar subject.

There are a number of reasons why this behavior rubs organizers the wrong way:

- It suggests that this is a sales and marketing effort and that the speaker's heart isn't in it.

- In my twelve years' experience, submissions of this kind are far more likely to cancel, renege, or try to substitute speakers—often, the suggested speaker isn't aware of the event and hasn't blocked off his or her calendar.

- Organizers often want to co-create a session by collaborating with the speaker, adjusting the description and tweaking the title for the audience. Not having contact information suggests that they're too busy or consider themselves too important to put in this kind of effort.

There's simply no good excuse not to include the presenter's contact information in the submission. As organizers, we're used to dealing with busy, important people and will be respectful of their time. And we'll gladly work with assistants and agencies to work out details. But if we can't reach the speaker, we assume they don't want to hear from us.

Jargon

The book *Made To Stick*[2] talks about the Curse of Knowledge—a problem that plagues marketers who know too much about their products or services. They're unable to empathize with someone who doesn't know as much as they do. They can't explain their offering without resorting to buzzwords and inside-industry slang.

If the submission is full of jargon, we assume that the presentation will be, too. Jargon may be acceptable for very technical talks to an audience of peers, but even then it suggests you can't simplify and synthesize ideas and that your message will be too specific to your own world to be of interest to others.

Get someone who doesn't know what you do to review your submission. Would this person be interested in it? Does he or she understand what you're saying? Can he or she explain it back to you? If not, consider rewording it with the reader and audience in mind.[3]

Sounding Like SkyMall

Ever read the descriptions in in-flight catalogs? "This is the prelit waterproof wreath decorated with ten realistic fabric poinsettias!" Their tone suggests that the product they're describing is somehow the only one of its kind in the world and that the reader is already acquainted

---

2. *http://www.heathbrothers.com/madetostick/*

3. And please take the time to watch "Hardly Working: Start-up Guys" at CollegeHumor.com (*http://www.collegehumor.com/video/6507690/hardly-working-start-up-guys*)—if you sound like this to others, start again.

with the product, no matter how obscure ("This is the automatic os-cillating table tennis trainer . . . ").

If you find these irritating, you're not alone. Reviewers find this kind of language smug, assumptive, and narcissistic. If your description says something like, "<Company> is *the* trusted provider of software, managed service, and cloud security products that help organizations secure their websites against hacker attacks,"[4] then you're telling the reader that you can't empathize with an audience that hasn't already drunk your Kool-Aid and that your presentation will be awkward and dull.

Trying to Change at the Last Minute

A session at an event consists of three things: a speaker, a topic, and a format. Changing any of these once you've been chosen is grounds for immediate rejection. The submission was chosen for the speaker and his or her ability to entertain, educate, and inspire.

There are three reasons that companies substitute a speaker:

- **They no longer work for the company**. If they were dismissed for a felony or something else that undermines their legitimacy as an expert, this may be a valid excuse. But unless their presentation is specifically about the organization for which they work, remember that we didn't choose them because of their employer, but rather because they know their subject matter and are good at communicating it. That didn't change the moment they left their job. I've often kept speakers, even though they went to work at a competitor, over the protests of the company that originally submitted the talk. *We want the person*, not the company they represent.

- **They have a scheduling conflict**. This just means they didn't plan well ahead or never intended to be at the conference. If you're slated to speak, don't schedule something else. Conferences are multimillion-dollar events that take months to plan. If you drop the ball, assume that you won't be chosen for future events: *before, we knew little about you, but now, we know you're unreliable.*

---

4. Yes, all three of these examples are real quotes. Unfortunately.

- **They have a genuine emergency**. This is the only real reason to change. We've had companies put a high-ranking executive on a red-eye flight to make a speaking engagement when one of their colleagues couldn't make it, which earned them high praise and repeat invitations.

 Make sure it's a real emergency. One conference organizer explains: "A company begged us to substitute a speaker, claiming the original speaker was incapacitated. But later that day, we saw the person actively chatting with attendees via social networks and checking in at restaurants. Needless to say, the company hasn't been chosen to present since."

Expecting to Be Paid, or Have Travel Paid For

Unless you have an arrangement with the event or the conference has a policy of paying speakers that's explained in the submission form, assume that there's no compensation for the event. The only speakers who get paid are those whom the organizers reach out to.

Nothing is more irritating than accepting a speaker only to have them renege on the invitation because they can't afford the travel. If you can't make the event, please don't waste the organizers' time submitting a session. If the conference doesn't state its travel policy on the submission page, it's almost certain you're responsible for your own travel and accommodations.

Proposing a Subject Too Narrow to Capture an Audience's Attention

Empathy is a big part of submitting the right topic. If your topic is too specific, there won't be enough attendees to justify the space at the conference and organizers will put a topic with broader appeal in there instead.

This is a tricky balance to strike. If you speak about something too broad ("mobile phones," for example), it'll be hard for attendees to self-select, because the subject applies to everyone but doesn't afford new knowledge or early insight into a field. On the other hand, if you speak about something nascent or overly narrow ("optimizing cell phone antennas on a Nokia N95 to maximize reception on ferry crossings in Norway"), you won't have the interest needed to attract an audience.

The goal here is to find a topic that has *information arbitrage* for the *broadest audience*. The more niche the subject, the fewer people will care about your expertise. The broader your subject, the less likely it is that you have special or unique knowledge.

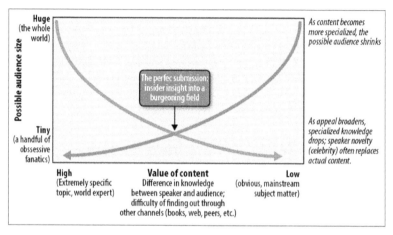

Figure 3-4. The trade-off between broad appeal and valuable content

You can create insider insight (moving to the left in Figure 3-4) by doing primary research, sharing otherwise secret data, or helping to share customer information that wouldn't normally be available. You can broaden your appeal (moving to the right in Figure 3-4) by attaching your niche topic (say, security risks of long-battery-life devices) to something broader (the rise of the coffee-shop mercenary worker).

Remember, too, that the subject has to be interesting on paper so that attendees will choose your session over others being run at the same time. The description has to sell the session to the audience as well as the organizers.

Bad Spelling, Formatting, and Punctuation

As organizers, we don't have many clues about what it'll be like to work with you or what your communications skills are. Organizers need to triage hundreds of submissions, and we're often guilty of a cognitive bias known as the Halo and Horns bias: once we see a single strength or flaw, we often judge the whole person based on this.

One of the main cues we have is the quality of the submission. Bad grammar, punctuation mistakes, and incorrectly used words suggest that you may be hard to work with, leading to misunderstandings and confusion around logistics. Worse, they suggest that you may not be a native speaker of the language in which the conference is run and that attendees will have a hard time following what you're saying.

Take the time to review a submission carefully. You may be a superb speaker with a great topic, but if your submission has mistakes, we'll assume that you do, too.

Submitting a Book

Although organizers need to know what you'll talk about, a long submission, such as a five-page résumé, is a sign that you don't know how to synthesize and summarize. If you're simply going to regurgitate content, the audience may as well read a white paper instead. Your role as a speaker is to interpret, enlighten, and offer new perspectives on the material, putting them in context.

Pick your three best, most important points. Write one to three sentences—no more—on each. List the three people who should attend and the five things they will learn. Add one sentence about the speaker. Then make sure that the title reflects what you've written. You don't need much more to convey what you're offering, and it will be easier for organizers to evaluate it. It's also more likely that what you've written will wind up in the conference materials unedited.

A Bad Past Experience (Not Showing Up, Reneging on a Submission)

Organizers have long memories, and all of them keep blacklists of those who are persona non grata based on past mistakes. There are simply too many great speakers to choose from to give someone a second chance. Just as a good speaker will get asked back, shared among organizers, and invited to other conferences, so too will a problem speaker develop a reputation.

Agencies are guilty of bad behavior, too: complaining about not being chosen; repeatedly and angrily demanding an explanation for why a competitor was selected; submitting sessions after the CFP has closed;

and pinging organizers to find out whether their client is in before the conference schedule is announced.

 One senior executive was scheduled to deliver a closing session at a conference. For two hours, the speaker coordinator tried to reach him by every means possible—email, cell phone, and his peers in the company—to no avail. Then, three minutes before the session was scheduled to start, he mailed us to say he had a conflict and wouldn't be able to attend.

He wasn't even in the same city.

I wound up racing to the room where he was supposed to speak, giving a quick overview of the subject matter, and engaging the audience in a roundtable discussion. The conversation wound up being fascinating, and the attendees rated the content well. But they rated the intended speaker horribly. Needless to say, he hasn't been invited back.

This is a bad list to be on if you're a professional speaker or an agency. It's much less likely that you'll be invited to participate or called on to speak on panels or join advisory boards. The only solution to this problem is to have a frank talk with organizers, but they're likely too busy to spend time with you if they've had bad experiences in the past.

We're willing to forgive the occasional problem. But the cardinal sin —the one that will get you banned for life—is disappointing an audience. If we get bad feedback from an audience or if you show up unprepared, switch topics on us, or generally lower the quality of the conference content, you're simply not coming back.

It's a good idea to handle rejection gracefully, too. This isn't personal. Phil Telio, organizer of Startup-camp and the International Startup Festival, says, "I have been blasted by speakers I've rejected. This is a sure way to never get invited to speak at a future event. Ever.

"There are some things you can do, however. Gracefully accepting rejection—and bothering to find out why—sets you up for the next event. And making me feel like I've missed something special is fine; I always do when there are only a limited number of spots. Offering to be a backup speaker is a great way to overcome rejection. Scheduled speakers have been known to cancel."

CHAPTER 4

Some Thoughts on Superb Presentations

What It Takes to Stand Out

I began by saying this isn't a book on how to present; it's a book on how to be *invited* to present. But once you've been invited, there's still plenty that can go wrong. With that in mind, here are some things to think about if you want to wow audiences and get invited back by organizers.

What Speaking Consultants Do

Some companies employ third-party speaking consultants to help them find speaking slots. The worst of these consultants simply spam the speaking circuit with boilerplate text, hoping for a bite. Chances are good that if you're using one of these agencies, you'll get to speak at only low-quality events at which attendees aren't good prospects or partners anyway.

On the other hand, the best consultants help you to become a better, more interesting, more connected participant in the conference ecosystem. One consultant I spoke with spends a lot of time with clients before submitting them, trying to find what's interesting about the firm and then mapping this to the events for which it's the best fit.[1]

---

1. Thanks to Deb Moses at Speaknow, Inc.; the folks at S3; and several other firms for giving us a candid look at what they do.

Here's what these kinds of consultants do:

- **Interview the company**. Before creating any proposals, they spend time interviewing company employees. They often avoid sales and marketing types, working instead with engineers, product managers, and even customers to understand what the organization does and what makes it unique. This process also helps them to find the diamonds in the rough within an organization, experts who are charming or knowledgeable but might not often be used as speakers.

- **Know the event**. As we've seen, each event has a narrative, a history, and a specific style. Knowing which events the company fits helps. If the speaker's company is informal, casual, and open, then they'll work best in an unbuttoned, less structured context. If they're businesslike and precise, they'll do better at more professional events.

- **Build relationships with the organizers**. These consultants work gently over years to try and understand the individual organizers and track chairs. The trick, for them, is to keep themselves and their clients in the minds of organizers without becoming a nuisance.

- **Co-create the content**. The consultants are familiar with the event and willing to adapt content. They can act as an ambassador between the story the organizer is trying to tell and the message the speaker wants to convey. This co-creation—rather than warring over sessions and titles—is often key to being included in an event.

- **Make it easy**. There are plenty of logistical details that need to be worked out between event organizers and speakers. Getting titles, biographies, photos, travel logistics, and timings straight is often a full-time job. Consultants know this, and they can lubricate the process.

Speaker consultant Deb Moses has the following recommendations for her clients:

- Don't: Create abstracts in a vacuum (meaning with input from only your own internal folks).

- Do: Review last year's program to see what topics were run, how technical- or business-oriented they were, the appropriate level of speaker, tone, and so on.

- Do: Bounce some ideas off the organizer first (in email) if possible.

- Don't: Recycle press materials or collateral.

- Do: Interview the prospective speaker and leverage white papers or technical papers with meaty content.

Avoiding the Almost-Awesome

As an organizer, one of my biggest frustrations is the *almost-awesome* submission. While reviewing several hundred submissions for a recent event, I had to read through nearly 20 sessions from the same vendor. Most were rejected immediately; the sheer volume of submissions exhausted us.

One session caught my eye. It was about anonymous authentication, a way to prove your identity without revealing personal data. At first, it seemed like a sales pitch. But as I read it, I thought, "Where is the average citizen subject to the most scrutiny?" When they cross a border, of course. And border guards are increasingly using social networks like Foursquare and Twitter to dig deeper into someone's travel history, seeing if you went where you said you did or if you're traveling on legitimate business.

That's a *fascinating* subject, rife with ethical and legal concerns. We give up hard-won rights to privacy at borders, and there's a tension between national security (this is the perimeter defense of a nation at war with terrorists) and personal freedom (why is it the government's business what its citizens do abroad?).

For example, the United States is considering revising legislation to state that a citizen violating domestic drug laws while overseas (i.e., visiting a coffee shop in Amsterdam) can be charged with a violation of domestic law. What if a border guard sees you checked into the Green Door in the Red Light district and that's considered probable cause, which leads to a drug test?

Anonymous authentication? Boring. **The ethics of security and privacy? Compelling**.

A well-planned submission would seduce organizers, and ultimately audiences, because it would be about a related subject. The speaker would still make his or her points. Instead, the session was down-voted by reviewers as too much of a sales pitch and never saw the light of day.

On the other hand, a vendor of online services, security, and testing products took the stage at another event. He was a paid sponsor. But he never even mentioned his company. He opened by saying, "I'm going to tell you about the biggest cloud in the world. It's been around for a decade, and the people who run it are much, much better than you."

The audience was on the edge of its seats.

"It's a botnet called Storm, run by hackers and spammers, using hundreds of thousands of infected machines," he continued. He then went on to compare this hacker network to more traditional clouds, showing how Storm was bigger, and its operators more hard-core, than anything the audience had seen before.

For the rest of the event, the company's exhibit booth was mobbed. It gave the firm a chance to talk about its services, which are related to measuring clouds and securing networks.

Too Many Words

I hate slides with words. They're a huge warning sign that someone will be an awful presenter. Here's why:

- **The speaker's notes excuse**. Word-filled slides are a crutch for presenters who don't know their content. Your audience isn't in a remedial reading course. If all you're going to do is show up and read some slides for them, do us all a favor and put a PDF on your website instead.

- **The "more than I had time for" excuse**. Pascal and others have said, "I apologize that this letter is so long. I did not have the time to make it short."[2] Presentations that have lots of words are an attempt to share more information than you have time for—a sign you haven't honed your presentation to make a few points well. By doing so, you're asking your audience to multitask, listening to you while reading. They'll learn even less.

- **The handouts-for-later excuse**. Once, attendees got handouts of slides, and valued the content. Today, most conferences hand out materials electronically, so you can use the speakers' notes of your slides to add useful data or put it in hidden slides. But we also have URL shorteners: if you have more details, then just offer a memorable short URL at the end of your presentation and invite people to download it. If you've inspire them, you will—and you can track the impact of your presentation, too!

I've presented alongside "corporate" presenters who, after seeing my more image-heavy decks, have adjusted their content and loosened up, putting in humorous imagery. In every case, they've remarked that it's a welcome change that builds rapport with the audience and gets a laugh.[3]

Finding Your Inner Diamonds

Corporate marketers face an unfortunate catch-22. Their senior executives want the limelight and expect to get the speaking engagements. But they may be horrible speakers—there's likely someone funnier and more knowledgeable on a specific subject, elsewhere in the company. Marketers can either field the lackluster speaker or earn the wrath of vain executives by choosing someone interesting and capable.

At the same time, we live in a "share" world. Twenty years ago word processors became commonplace, and a decade ago we learned spreadsheets; today most professionals are expected to know their way around presenting tools like PowerPoint, Keynote, or Prezi. That means more employees are expected to present, either to an internal

---

2. *http://www.classy.dk/log/archive/001074.html* says that although it's commonly attributed to Twain, this joke goes far back, to Cicero, Augustin, and Pascal, among others.

3. Want an easy laugh? Use a meme generator. Go to *http://www.memecrunch.com* or something similar and create something funny and relevant to your subject.

audience or to an outside group. Although many people are terrified of public speaking, it's easy to overcome this fear with practice.

Traditionally, speakers honed their skills in friendly groups like Toastmasters. But today, events like Ignite and Pecha Kucha, unconferences, and websites such as TED showcase excellent presentations on hundreds of subjects.

If your company is serious about speaking in public and wants to invest in it, then you need to create ways to find and polish the rough diamonds in your midst. Ignite is perfect for this. It has a rigid presentation format that constrains the length of each speech. These constraints are surprisingly liberating, forcing speakers to focus on brevity and keeping the audience entertained. Here's how it works:

- A few weeks before the event, the organizer solicits volunteers who want to present. They may suggest a theme, although that isn't really necessary.
- Volunteers submit a title, and perhaps a synopsis, of their presentation.
- If chosen, those volunteers create a 20-slide, 5-minute deck. Each slide is shown for just 15 seconds and advances automatically.
- The volunteers rehearse. A lot. It's hard to extemporize when you can't control the clock.
- On the night of the event—these things are best held at night, with beer—each presenter gets up and delivers a five-minute rant, with little pause between speakers.

This is a great social activity for any organization: not only does it help you find great speakers, but it also gets everyone sharing their interests. It's also a great exercise for sales training meetings. It's such a tight format that things are bound to break, and everyone's supportive. And if someone's boring—well, it's only five minutes.[4]

A second way to break the presentation ice is PowerPoint Karaoke, the strange progeny of Ignite and Improv. In this exercise, presenters get a slide deck they've never seen before and have to present it. The deck is stacked for maximum humor, either as a compilation of random

---

4. To see examples of Ignite sessions, check out *http://www.igniteshow.com*; even if your organization can't run one, if you live in a big city there's probably one near you soon.

slides or as content from an unrelated field. It could even be a competitor's sales pitch. The point is that the presenter doesn't know what's coming next and has to make it up on the fly.

We've run PowerPoint Karaoke at a number of events, and it always makes people more comfortable when presenting. We've created fifteen or so slide decks for Bitnorth, and you can use SlideShare to generate them randomly, too.[5]

Both Ignite and PowerPoint Karaoke are fun, social formats. But they'll also help you find promising presenters in a safe, supportive environment. If your organization is serious about getting heard in public, start here.

Logistics and Polish

There are really only two rules when it comes to presenting. *Be comfortable speaking in public* and *practice your presentation.* If you can do these two things, you'll be fine. Of course, practicing doesn't just mean reading your presentation on the flight. You need to deliver it over and over again until you've made it your own.

Assuming you've taken this advice, here are some other tips that may help:

- Don't wear finely patterned clothing, as this can produce a moiré pattern[6] when recorded on video. Solid colors work best if you're being recorded.

- Whenever possible, use a headset microphone that provides the best audio signal. If you're nervous, people will see your hands shaking as you hold a handheld microphone, and you might accidentally point it at a speaker and generate ear-piercing feedback, deafening the room. Podium microphones keep you in one place and put something between you and your audience, making things look stiff and awkward.

- If you're using a lavaliere microphone (the ones clipped to your shirt), remember that the volume changes when you turn your head to the sides, and if you move around a lot, you might generate a rustling noise.

5. Check out *http://blog.slideshare.net/2007/07/11/slideshare-karoake-randomizer/*.
6. *http://en.wikipedia.org/wiki/Moir%C3%A9_pattern*

- If you're forced to use a handheld microphone, put it closer to your mouth than you think is necessary. This will make it easier for the sound technicians to get a good signal and reduce the chance of feedback. There's nothing more distracting than a mumbling, hard-to-hear panelist.

- Carry your own remote if you do this sort of thing often. Infrared remotes (sold with MacBooks) don't work well, as they need a line of sight between the computer and the remote; PDA-based remotes (such as Apple's Keynote remote) are hard to set up and require a wireless connection. Go with a simple, dedicated, wireless remote; they cost less than $100.

- Wipe your forehead and nose with a dry paper towel before taking the stage, to reduce glare and reflection.

- Start by polling the audience to break the ice and get a sense of who's there and what they hope to achieve. This approach also allows you to tailor your presentation on the fly and shows the audience that you care about them, not yourself.

- Include your Twitter handle, and other ways of reaching you, up front. This makes the audience more likely to mention you during and after the event and provides quick feedback as well as a way to follow up on leads.

- Avoid showing a video at all costs. Screening a movie is a crutch. That's what YouTube and Vimeo are for.

Speaker consulting firm S3 has the following recommendations for their clients:

- Do: Tell great stories, get to the point, practice, and use humor when possible.
- Do: Get training if you're expected to speak but are not comfortable doing so.
- Do: Start by speaking on panels to get comfortable with the process, the audience, and the event.
- Do: Move purposefully while speaking.
- Do: Close with a call to action.
- Don't: Sell, preach, or talk down.
- Don't: Use your slides' content as a crutch or as notes.
- Don't: Use vague words like "maybe" or "hope." Instead, be clear and decisive.
- Don't: Assume the audience from your last speech is the same as this one; spend time preparing and tailoring the content.

CHAPTER 5

But How Do I Make Money?

If you've read this far and you're in corporate marketing, you probably have one big objection: all of this is great and makes things interesting, but it doesn't accomplish your business goals—generating leads, closing sales, and making prospects aware of your product.

Engaging Before, During, and After

Presenting is inherently a one-way, one-to-many medium, more like television or newspapers than personal interaction. You can make it personal, however. Turning a monologue into a dialogue is step one in turning interest into a sale.

The first rule of selling from the stage is to leave them wanting more. The audience feels like part of a special group and gets privileged access; you seem less motivated by self-interest and more by a genuine desire to share. So find a way to tantalize and tease, then end by telling them how they can get what they're after.

- If you're putting your slides online, **include extra ones** that offer more detailed facts and figures, and mention this. Put in **speakers' notes that have extra information** or recap your speech. This way, regardless of where the slides are posted, your message goes along with them.

- When you post the content, do so on a site that offers **email updates or a mailing list** for folks who are interested. It's not generally a good idea to force people to register in order to download content—this kind of registration has poor conversion rates, and it feels like you're breaking the promise you made from the stage.

- Consider **using a slide-sharing service like SlideShare**, which allows embedding and management of your brand and lets you connect with readers who can recommend your content elsewhere.

- If you're sponsoring or exhibiting at the event, **invite people to the booth** to discuss some of the points you made, fill out a survey, or collect additional content.

There are many other ways to spark a discussion and track the impact of your presentation. If you want to track the influence your content is having or how much it's accessed, then **use a short URL** from a tool such as bit.ly as the last slide in your deck. If this short URL points to your content somewhere online, then you'll be able to measure how many people followed the link as a result of your presentation.

Open, unwalled social networks like Twitter and Google+ are searchable. If you **use a unique sentence** in your presentation, you're more likely to be able to search for it after the fact. One presenter we know goes so far as to put these pithy, short sentences on dedicated slides with a Twitter logo—urging attendees to tweet his nuggets of wisdom. It's even better to **use a particular hash tag** in your presentations as a place to carry on the discussion. If you can, have a colleague **tweet links that are in your slides** as you mention them on stage, using short URLs, with the event hash tag. You're doing attendees a favor by making it easy for them to find the resources you're discussing, and you can see exactly how popular those resources were.

A machine learning company that was attending a conference I ran decided to use their software to build a map of the key terms discussed at the conference and how they related to one another. They mentioned this on the event's hash tag, which was retweeted by the hosts, and received a huge amount of traffic.

After the conference, bloggers and attendees referred to their analysis. To this day, it's the most successful piece of marketing they've ever done, and it gave them considerable credibility and an easy introductory story to tell prospects.

You can also **survey the audience** using a number of open survey tools. Invite them to visit a link, ask them a few questions, and summarize the results in a blog post. You can even collect survey data *before* your presentation and then use it in the presentation itself. This method helps you better tailor what you're saying and can even contribute valuable insight to your market research efforts.

By all means, use a **discount code or special offer** in your conclusion. Just make sure it's extraordinary and worth talking about—make it time-limited, or restrict it to the first ten people, for example—so it feels like you're really offering something to the audience.

Finally, try to think like a pickup artist. **Say something provocative**, get a reaction, and then invite customers to continue the discussion on a social network or forum. Good marketers can turn engagement into conversion, and once you're connected to someone online, you'll know a lot about them.

Further Reading

Hopefully, you now have some insight into the mind of an event organizer and into how conferences are run. This is just the beginning: there are plenty of excellent books on speaking techniques, slide design, and creating great stories. Here are just a few:

- *Slideology* (O'Reilly), Nancy Duarte's excellent book on presentation design. Nancy also says plenty of smart things on her blog (*http://blog.duarte.com/*).

- *Made to Stick* (Random House), by Chip and Dan Heath, is perhaps one of the best marketing books of the last decade. It tackles being memorable and interesting as well as avoiding jargon and the curse of too much knowledge. It should be required reading for anyone setting foot on a stage. Find out more at *http://www.heathbrothers.com/madetostick/*.

- *Confessions of a Public Speaker (http://www.speakerconfes sions.com/)* (O'Reilly) by Scott Berkun gives you an inside look at what it's like to speak for a living. Scott's blog (*http://www.scott berkun.com/*) is a great resource.

- Solve for Interesting (*http://solveforinteresting.com/category/good-conference/*) is where I write about a variety of things; the Good Conferences category focuses on running events that don't suck.

- Ignite (*http://www.igniteshow.com*) and TED (*http://www.ted.com*) are filled with great examples of excellent presentations on compelling topics in five to twenty minutes.

- Tara Hunt's *How To Rock An Audience (http://www.slide share.net/missrogue/how-to-rock-an-audience-from-stage-fright-to-stage-presence)* has great guidelines on presenting well and overcoming stage fright.

About the Author

I've been helping to run conference events since 1998, focusing largely on the content side of things as an instructor and moderator. My allegiance is to the audience, which means I'm also a thorn in the side of sales teams and sponsors.

Five of the events I've been lucky enough to work with—O'Reilly Strata, Interop ECS, Cloud Connect, GigaOM Structure, and the International Startup Festival—sold out in their first year and have connected thousands of people over the years. Most of my great experiences have come from the people in those organizations taking a chance on me, and for that I'm immensely grateful.

Today, I'm the chair of O'Reilly's Strata conference, TechWeb's Cloud Connect conference, and the International Startup Festival. I've also helped organize the Decibel music festival, GigaOM's Structure, the SIIA's annual conference, a number of events on lean entrepreneurship, and a variety of others.

I'm pretty active in the Montreal tech community, helping to organize YULEtide/TechNoel, the RPM Startup space, the Year One Labs startup accelerator, hackathons, and local Ignite events. I also created Bitnorth, the antidote to traditional events—a rustic, unstructured, weekend-long event north of Montreal.

A product manager by trade, I've written four books on technology and startups, including *Lean Analytics (http://www.leananalytics book.com)* (O'Reilly). I co-founded Coradiant, a web performance monitoring company acquired by BMC Software in 2011, as well as Rednod, Bitcurrent, and Networkshop. I've presented at a number of tech events in North America, Europe, and the Middle East, and I act as an advisor to a few VC firms, helping them to better guess where technology is headed and why people should care about it.

Have it your way.

Get even more for your money.

Join the O'Reilly Community, and register the O'Reilly books you own. It's free, and you'll get:

- $4.99 ebook upgrade offer
- 40% upgrade offer on O'Reilly print books
- Membership discounts on books and events
- Free lifetime updates to ebooks and videos
- Multiple ebook formats, DRM FREE
- Participation in the O'Reilly community
- Newsletters
- Account management
- 100% Satisfaction Guarantee

Signing up is easy:

1. Go to: oreilly.com/go/register
2. Create an O'Reilly login.
3. Provide your address.
4. Register your books.

Note: English-language books only

To order books online:

oreilly.com/store

For questions about products or an order:

orders@oreilly.com

To sign up to get topic-specific email announcements and/or news about upcoming books, conferences, special offers, and new technologies:

elists@oreilly.com

For technical questions about book content:

booktech@oreilly.com

To submit new book proposals to our editors:

proposals@oreilly.com

O'Reilly books are available in multiple DRM-free ebook formats. For more information:

oreilly.com/ebooks

Spreading the knowledge of innovators   oreilly.com

Milton Keynes UK
Ingram Content Group UK Ltd.
UKHW021830131123
432501UK00012B/312